Simply
from
the
Heart

Poems and Prayers
by
Annamae Cameron

Copyright © 2022 Tuesday Night Publishing

ISBN 978-0-9989032-3-1
Printed in the Unites States of America
First Printing, 2022

As a child, I was amused by my dad's funny little rhymes. I started saying them back to him. It was a sweet connection we had. I wrote verses and poetry to my parents expressing my love. My dad always encouraged me to write poetry. He was a poet.

I constantly journaled and expressed my thoughts and love to God in this way. My love of poetry grew as I got older. I especially loved Helen Steiner Rice and Annie Johnson Flint. My favorite of all was King David and his Psalms. Through poetry, I found much peace, comfort, and pleasure in expressing myself to God.

"Simply from the Heart" is a collection of poems and prayers from my heart to God. It is up close and personal, inspired by the Holy Spirit, family, friends, and nature. I hope the simplicity and honesty touch your heart.

The paintings are a few selected pieces of my artwork. I love nature because I love the creator. Oil painting was a hobby I picked up as a young mother. It soothed my soul.

I hope you enjoy it and that it brings peace and comfort to your soul.

-Annamae Cameron

This book is lovingly dedicated to:

Father God, who calls me beautiful daughter.

Jesus Savior and dearest friend.

Holy Spirit, my comforter, inspiration, and constant companion.

My husband, Tim, my hero!

My children: Joe, Tina, Elizabeth, Rachael, and Stephen; the gems in my crown.

My sons-in laws: Jared and James, answers to prayer.

My goddaughters: Tori and Sophia, sweet additions.

My grandchildren: Isaac, Camie, Sammy, JJ, Ellie, Gabe, and Micah; my treasured gifts.

To all my dear, precious friends and relatives. Especially Lea and Martine, for your love and encouragement.

Acknowledgment and thanks to Joe and Matt, my editors.

Grandchild

Oh little grandchild, please come to my heart,
I know you're waiting in heaven for this life to start.
Oh is it true? Could it be, God is forming you for me!
Oh the joy and happiness I feel inside;
Anticipating your arrival on earth to abide.
Will you have brown eyes or will they be blue?
Will you wear pretty pink gowns
or gritty, blue tennis shoes?
God is so good, His word is true,
He promised me a grandchild, and that grandchild is you.

The Last Reunion

We gathered together one last time to celebrate our love,
heritage, and commitment to each other.
We remember our growing up years, the fun,
and our godly father and mother.
Though our parents are gone, we tenderly remember them
with stories, laughter, and song.
Time is passing by too fast and the day will soon be gone.
We take our pictures, chat, and play
and to God give our praise.
We wish time would stand still awhile
so together we could stay.
We hug each other and say our goodbyes,
trying so hard not to cry.
Will we ever be together like this again?
My dear siblings who are my friends,
There is a time coming when it's our final goodbye.
For one of us will go ahead
to our heavenly home in the sky.
Then we will wait for the greatest reunion of them all.
Where we will all be together again
with mom and dad standing tall.
But today together we will celebrate the life
as siblings we had.
Making sweet memories, playing, praying, and sharing;
in our hearts, we are so glad.

Me

When you see a sunset or the crashing of the waves,
The chirping of the cardinal,
And the beauty of snowy days,
That's when I want you to think of me.
My life in Jesus was so free.
I loved the beautiful sunsets.
His presence there, I met.
I loved the ocean and walking barefoot on the sand.
Jesus walking with me, holding my hand.
I loved the beautiful cardinals watching them chirp and play;
God's beautiful creation for us He displays.
I loved to watch the snow fall on cold winter days,
Reminding me of Jesus' blood that washes my sins away.

Dive Deep

Dive deep beneath the crashing waves
that hold us in its twisting grip;
Tumbling and tossing a breathless beating we submit.
Dive deep into the silence and stillness
that calms our body and soul.
Sheltering us from the turbulence
above that holds such control.
When the waves start to break upon us
and no safety in sight,
Dive deep into the silent stillness
where HE shines HIS light.
The crashing and turbulence will pass over
and you're safe from its snare.
You learned to dive deep and rest in HIS love and care.

Silent Tears

My heart is crying silent tears day and night
For all the pain and suffering hidden and in sight,
For the aborted babies who will not live,
Their mothers who would not give,
The homeless man in despair,
The rich man who did not share,
For the one suffering with disease and pain;
In Your grace and mercy, let them find gain.
Oh God, oh God, my heart breaks in two,
For this hurting world, if only they knew.
Silent tears day and night,
I enter intercession to declare Your hope and love in this fight.
May all my actions share your love and light;
Silent tears day and night, intercession is this fight.

The Cross

Holding tight to The Cross of Christ
Where the tree makes the bitter water sweet.
Holding tight to The Cross of Christ
Where I bow down at my savior's feet.

When despair and hopelessness knock at my door,
Holding tight to The Cross makes my heart soar.
When pain and brokenness is all that I see,
Holding tight to The Cross is where I'll be.
When tears and mourning blind my sight,
That's when the grip becomes very tight,
Holding me to The Cross of Christ.

Holding tight to The Cross of Christ
As his blood washes over my soul.
Holding tight to The Cross of Christ
Where his love does make me whole.

My Sweet Love

Bless You, my dear sweet, sweet Lord.
There are no words to describe how
Precious you are, how adored.

Consume me, my sweet, sweet love.
Take my breath away, steal my heart,
Go deep and touch every part.

My yearning for You is so strong.
Fill me, my Lord, engulf my soul.
Be my sweet, sweet love song.

Break through my hard heart.
Crush it, consume it, tear it all apart,
Then hold it, mold it, and make it new,
A heart wholly, totally all for you.
Always be my sweet, sweet Love,
Wooing me, loving me, like a gentle dove.

I've never known a love so strong,
One that has captured me for so long.
This kind of love is oh so rare,
Sweet, consuming, so deeply cared.
Bless You, my dear, sweet, sweet Lord,
You're my true love, the one I adore.

A Mother

Once a mother,
always a mother all of your life,
When they're a baby or teen,
and when they're a wife.

Seasons come, seasons go,
and mother is always staking care:
Giving, loving, praying,
with Godly advice to share.

It doesn't matter what state you're in,
if in trials or delight;
Mother is always there for you,
until matters are made right.

When you're a mother,
then you'll know the binding love that's there,
Always and forever you'll love, pray, and care.

Then the day will come that mother will be gone,
But her love and care will still be there
in your heart, with a tender song.

A Marriage Prayer

Heal our hearts and help us never to blame;
Holy Spirit come and on us rain.

Break away hardness and despair;
Keep us with a heart of love that cares.

Let Your love rule in our hearts,
Instead of hardness that would tear us apart.

Keep us focused on that sweet, tender love
That smiled down on us from heaven above.

Touch us now of any hurt or pain;
Always let forgiveness in us reign.

Humble our hearts, as to You we yield;
This is our prayer, to You we appeal.

Let us always remember the sweet, tender times,
When traveling and dating our love we did find.

Help us not let the pressures of life,
with all its trouble and all its strife,

Rob us of that sweet, tender plant growing in love—
please water and enhance.

This is our prayer, oh Lord, we say:
pour Your mercy and grace on us today.

Suffering

Bruised and broken and tossed about
like a boat on a turbulent sea,
The pain and suffering are taking its toll,
constantly battering me.

When will it cease?
When will it end?
How long can this stress I stand?
You promised not to give me
more than I could bear and
that angels would hold me in their hands.

Thank you, Lord, for holding me up
in this trial of suffering and pain;
Only in Your mercy and grace
can my life find in You its gain.

Night

In the night hours, You visit me, so sweet,
Ministering health and peace while I sleep.

Touching my heart and piercing my soul,
While I sleep, You make me whole.

When I awake, I'm refreshed and made new,
Because I have spent the night being loved by You.

Bitterness

When bitterness came knocking at my door,
I asked, "What are you here for?"

"I came to hold you in your misery and pain;
Life is unjust and unfair, nothing for you to gain."

I crumpled and cried, wondering what should I do:
Let this stranger hold me or turn to the One who's true?

I chose Jesus, whose comfort and grace is real;
In His arms of mercy, His love does heal.

Then I saw His good complete plan;
He has always held me close in His hand.

Now I have such compassion for all in need;
Jesus worked His life in me, and on His word I will feed.

Hidden Places

Hidden places are where life begins,
Sweet and pure without sin.

Hidden places deep within my heart,
Where You abide and set me apart.

Hidden places down in the soil,
The oak tree and rose bush start their toil.

Hidden places, the caterpillar makes its way,
To become beautiful and fly away.

Hidden places in You is where I long to be,
So all things spectacular, I can see.

Where the veil comes down and I am free,
Hidden places—just You and me.

My Dear Love

Heal me, my dear love,
hold me in your arms where I want to be.
Let the fire of your love burn through me,
Healing, delivering, and setting me free.
My dear love who is always there for me,
I want to be a bride who has no soil on her gown;
Washed by Your blood, wooed by Your love,
hearing Your love's sweet sound.
Be so near; Holy Spirit, please come,
Comforting, helping, teaching me to be like God's son.
My dear love, Holy Spirit, please come.

No Respecter of Persons

It doesn't matter who I am or how successful I've been.
Your love and presence pours out to me,
and Your blood covers all my sin.

It doesn't matter how fashionable I am or what I wear,
Your love and presence covers me,
and I will always feel Your care.

It doesn't matter my state of affairs, rich, poor, slave or free.
Your presence and life are always a part of me.

It doesn't matter who my friends are or what job I have.
Your presence always comforts me and is a healing salve.

You are no respecter of persons;
there is no rank or social status you require.
Your presence draws my heart and life,
and Your love takes me higher.

Your presence pours out freely to all
who come to You in spirit and in truth.
You are no respecter of persons,
whether old or in their youth.

Know Me

Do You think I'm pretty?
Do You think I'm grand?
Do You like to look at me?
Do You want to hold my hand?

I need Your approval;
I need Your gaze
To get me through
The hard and lonely days.

Do You know what I'm thinking?
Do You know how I feel?
Will You hold me close
From the winter's chill?

Lord, You're so beautiful to me.
It's Your face that I long to see.
All I want to do is stay close to Thee,
Abide in Your presence, and in Your word feed.

Arrows

Arrows pierce my soul,
And they hurt so bad;
One day you're happy,
The next you're sad.

The gossip and slander,
That arrow went so deep;
It pierced my heart
And made me weep.

Holy Spirit, take these arrows out
And heal my wounded soul;
For in You, healing waters flow
Where I'll walk fresh and be made whole.

Holy Spirit, put my shield of faith
In its proper place,
So when the arrows come
I just step aside with grace.

Friend

Friend is a word of a linguist's delight;
Friend is a masterpiece—its brilliance sheds light.
Friend is a word of a Godly tone;
Friend is excellence standing alone.
Friend describes the ultimate bond;
Friend sung is the sweetest song.
Friend is always faithful and true;
Friend dear to me, I've found in you.

Take Time

Do you take time to smell the roses
As you pass by,
Or behold the beautiful sunset
In the evening sky?

Do you take time to walk the dogs
And greet the neighbors along the way,
Or visit your elderly friend
Who's shut in for the day?

Do you take time to call your loved one or friend
And encourage them in their need,
Or send a little offering
To help the hungry feed?

Do you take time to thank God
For His goodness and His love,
Or for sending Jesus to us
From heaven above?

Time is a vapor that's passing by fast;
This moment on Earth is not going to last.
So take time to enjoy life to its fullest and give;
In so doing, you will have really lived.

Lead Me

Lead me, Lord, to that lonely man
Who's in need of a helping hand.

Lead me, Lord, to that hurting mom
Who needs saving from the sinking sand.

Lead me, Lord, to the broken hearted,
Where a kind word will heal,
And Your loving touch can give a fresh start.

Lead me, Lord, to walk in Your way,
Where grace, truth, and mercy make up my day.

The Secret Place

The secret place of God surrounds me
When in my pain and sorrow I bow.

My mind can't comprehend it;
It's a mystery—how?

His love and comfort wash over me
Like a breaking wave.

He takes me deep into His secret place;
It's like a healing cave.

My pain is erased and sorrow rested
When sitting as His feet.

The secret place of God
Where always we will meet.

Antidote

Such sorrow on this Earth,
A heart can no longer bear.

Murder, hatred, and divorce;
Is there really a God who cares?

My wondering took me far and wide
Seeking truth to share.

I found an old, old story,
Do I believe it—do I dare?

It's of a love so radical,
He gave His life for me.

He took the sins of this Earth,
And showed me Calvary.

Now I share this wonderous love
To all in their need.

I point all to Jesus
Where His love will set you free.

Grace

Grace is my friend;
I love her embrace so much.
She enables me to go way beyond
My abilities with a gentle touch.

Grace is my friend;
Her companionship so dear.
She promises to stay with me
Always so near.

Grace is my friend,
So comforting and kind;
A gift from the Holy Spirit
That will always be mine.

My Hands

My hands are worn and old;
The scars seen on my skin.
The secrets they do hide;
The stories they do rend.

The callouses do speak of
The hard work and the toil
Laboring, lifting, and planting seed
In the hard, cool soil.
The scar across the thumb,
Speaks of mischievous deeds;
I should've listened to Mom's advice
And her wisdom heed.

The freckles on the skin
Speak of love of sun and sea;
The whispering of the waves
In my heart will always be

The dent from the wedding ring
Shows of a deep, true love,
With decades of blessing
Showered from above.

The softness of the fingertips
Wiped away baby's tears,
While the patting of the palm
So soothed a toddler's fears.

The tenderness they showed
While my babies I did hold,
Turning the pages of a book
While to them stories are told.

The gentle soothing love and care
To my children these hands did give,
Taking every heartache
And all their burdens bear.

The redness shows the spankings
That at times were required;
I'm so glad these hands are old
And from that act retired.

These hands did serve many with
The giving and kind deeds;
May God always use them,
And to Jesus many lead.

These hands are worn and old
But handled life with grace;
For my eyes were focused on my sweet Savior's face,
His nail-scarred hands I did embrace.

In Remembrance of You

I remember Your gift of Jesus,
born in a manger, Your gift of love.
You sent Him for us
From his kingdom above.

I remember His life
That He dwelled and walked among men
Healing us, touching us, loving us;
There is no end.

I remember His death
And dying on the cross
To cleanse us, forgive us;
He created us not loss.

This I do in remembrance of You,
I take the bread and the wine;
I am so grateful that Your life
Lives in me divine.

Dance of Love

Let's dance a while my faithful friend,
My love, my companion to the very end.
We'll dance on the clover soft
While the sun shines high;
You'll hold me, twirl me,
And teach me to fly.
We'll dance over
The rocky, thorny ground;
You'll hold me up
And never put me down.
Your dance of love has set me free;
We'll dance forever through eternity.

Joy Marie

Joy Marie, you were the most beautiful baby at your birth.
Joy Marie, you were too young to leave this earth.
You were only with us twenty-eight years;
Now we are all left with countless tears.
How beautiful you looked on your wedding day;
Just a few short years—with us you couldn't stay.
How can we make it?
Through God's sweet comfort and love.
We can look into the heavens
And know you're just above.
We will miss you, sweet Joy Marie,
But together we'll be through eternity.
So we'll say goodbye for now;
God's grace will show us how.

All Yours

Lift this fog from my eyes and let me see
Your purpose, my freedom, and all You have for me.

Clear my thoughts and all that comes to mind,
That my life would reflect You and brightly shine.

Tune my ears to hear Your still, sweet voice
Guiding me and helping me make the right choice.

Let my words bring You all the glory
While speaking kindness, love, and the gospel story.

Bless all that You give my hands to do,
Helping and serving others as unto You.

Keep my feet that they might not stumble
By walking upright and being humble.

Cleanse, soften, and heal this heart;
I give it all to You, every part.

I'm Yours, Lord—my body, mind, and soul.
In Your love and presence, I'll always be whole.

Jesus, Our Burdens to Bear

As we toil down life's journey,
there seems to be no end
To all the burdens, grief,
and heartache to family and friends.

So we turn our eyes to Jesus, the one who truly cares;
Sweet Jesus takes it all, our burdens to bear.

He promises not to give us more
than our weak hearts can stand;
In the midst of all the suffering,
He keeps us focused on His plan.

Our hope is not on things of Earth that only fade away,
But on Jesus, our rock, our hope will ever stay.

More

There has got to be more of Your life in me;
There has got to be more, so others can see
The cleansing Blood of Calvary.
So mankind can be set free,
There has got to me more of Your life in me.
I'll take up my cross, daily it will be,
So Your life in me, others can see.
I long for your Holy Spirit's fire in me to burn,
So the lame will walk and the sinner will turn.
I'll gladly lay down my life for a friend;
I'll walk the narrow path to the very end,
Because You shed Your blood and cleansed me from sin.
I love You, dear Lord, and I will always long
For more of Your life in me to be strong.

Simply Yours

Some may say I'm simple, and that's okay with me.
No shopping at Saks, but Wal-Mart instead;
my pies are from the apple tree.

I like the simple things in life:
sitting by the fire or walking with a friend;
To all the simple pleasures, there is no end.

I love the beautiful sunsets and walking by the sea
With your hand in mine, Lord, keeping me company.

I'm simply Yours, Lord, all the way around;
I see Your face in nature, and in its simple sounds.

I love my little doggies, and all the Christmas lights,
The dew on the roses, and the silvery moon at night.

It's all so simple,
But it's my greatest delight.

I love my warm bed on a cold wintery night
And the warmth of my husband holding me so tight.

I love all my children at home around the Christmas tree
Loving, laughing, and playing in sweet harmony.

When I serve you dinner, it might be on paper plates;
Bone China or not, my love is just as great.

I love to hear the Christmas songs, "Away in a Manger,"
"Jingle Bells," and "You Better not Pout,"
Whether sang by angelic choirs
or The Beach Boys with a shout.

You may think I'm simple, that's pretty plain to see;
That's perfectly okay—Jesus made me.

My English might not be the best,
But my words of encouragement will give you rest.

I might be unmannered in the ways of the elite,
But if you'll let me, I'll gladly wash your feet.

Who is this person, you might surely want to know;
If you give me a chance, true friendship will show.

Life Pages

Like the turning of a page, one life will surely pass;
Whatever we have, whatever we do, none of it will last.

Write on your page with purpose,
and write on your page with grace;
The pages keep on turning, so there is no time to waste.

Make sure your ink is dark enough
and your message written right;
Make sure your inspiration comes from the One True Light.

When the final words are written and I lay my pen down,
I'll place my hand in His hand, the truest friend I've found.

And when you read my book, the one theme that you'll see
Is God's Holy Spirit was burning inside me.

A Heart Like Mom

Mom, did it pain you deeply when all us children left the nest?
Or was it sweet relieving, and you could get some rest?

Did your heart hurt with a longing
to hold your babies once again?
Or did you fill it with walking and talking with a friend?

Mom, were the holidays and vacations with us enough?
Were you able to handle our absence
with other meaningful stuff?

Mom, I know how you survived us being gone;
You filled it with praise and prayers for us
and a beautiful song.

Now my children are all saying goodbye;
They don't see all the tears running down my eyes.

But they will feel my prayers, praise, and all my love,
Because God gave me a heart like yours,
Mom, a heart from heaven above.

The Choice

When life is full of disappointment,
and love has missed its mark,
When those you love are gone
and the night is too long and dark,
What do you do in that hour that surely clouds the soul?
Do you turn your eyes to Jesus,
whose truth can make you whole?

Tribulation comes to all of us, in one form or the other;
Do you hide away in seclusion or reach out to a brother?
Perseverance comes to all of us who learn to trust and wait;
Can you choose better not bitter? Can you love and not hate?

When the veil is finally lifted and eternity we'll see,
"Well done Thy faithful servant," for you will that be?

Choose you this day whom you will serve,
the choice will always be there:
To live for your selfish desires or for Jesus love and care.

Which will it be for you? Can you forgive without attack?
Can you go on down the road without the payback?

Do you hold onto your injustice and nurse it like a child?
Do you want to retaliate, then the mess becomes wild.

If you choose not to forgive, the cost will be great.
Remember with God, it's never too late;
Choose Christ and open heaven's gate!

Today

Enjoying the present, that's all we have;
The past is over and gone.

The future may never come,
Too many things that can go wrong.

So live for today, wholly and true
With earnest and gust in all that you do.

Looking ahead is a waste of time;
Too many hurtles you see to climb.

Shed the past, it's too heavy to bear;
There's no profit in it to even care.

Today is the day that the Lord hath made
To live in, laugh in, and for no other day trade.

Come This Night

Maybe You will come this night;
What excitement fills my soul!

Oh, the beauty of Your sight;
What a marvel to behold!

Maybe You will come this night;
God says, "Son, it's time!"

The heavens will open up in light;
The brightness my eyes will blind!

Maybe You will come this night;
The trumpet sound so clear!

My body will gladly rise in flight;
Heaven's choir will sing and cheer!

Maybe You will come this night;
My hope will always be!

The time is oh so ripe,
To live with you eternally!

Balm of Gilead

There is a balm of Gilead that washes over my soul
Going into every crack and crevice
and making the broken whole.

There is a balm of Gilead, it's the oil of God's love;
It brings healing to my hurt and pain
and His comfort from above.

There is a balm of Gilead, it's so soothing and complete;
I feel His aroma around me as I bow at His feet.

There is a balm of Gilead that calms the rage in me;
Only the miracle of His grace sets my spirit free.

Hopeless and Afraid

Are you hopeless and full of despair?
Has life left you with no one to care?
Are you broken inside,
Emptied of pride?
Has life totally let you down,
And no loyal love have you found?
Are your eyes dry from all the tears you've cried?
Do people just pass by
Not seeing all the hurt and pain?
Do you wonder what happened to your
Plans of wealth and fame?
When everything has crumbled down
And dust is all you see,
Is it true? Could it be possible?
Is there a God who really loves me?
Where is He? Can He take this mess I've made?
Can He put me back together? Will He stay?
All I do is give Him my heart!
Its broken and torn all apart;
He'll take it, remake it, and new it will be.
He will really come and live in me.
What kind of God have I discovered?
Like Him above or beneath, there is no other.
How can a God come and live in me?
It's really possible through Calvary.
Who was this Jesus who bled and died?
God's Son, the Three-In-One—
Wow, it's a miracle that's hard to believe;
But truth speaks loudly, and my spirit is free.

A New Heart

Oh, wrecked heart, who can know the sin
And wickedness you show,
And how the roots go deep and grow.
Oh, wrecked heart, how blind I've been;
Tormented, crippled in my sin;
Needing a Savior more than a friend.
Oh, wrecked heart, so hard and black,
The God in heaven will claim you back;
Thorough, complete in Him no lack.
Oh, wrecked heart, God's love will break;
The blood of Jesus will cleanse and remake;
All that's lost, He will retake.
Oh, beautiful heart, now brand new,
Full of God's love, all for You.
Oh, beautiful heart, in God I live
Obedient and true; all to Him I give.

Growing Old Grace

Growing old, grace we abundantly need,
For all the quirks and changes that will eventually be.

The brow in the chin, the faded out grin,
The wobbly step and the knees that don't bend.

Growing old, grace we abundantly need,
For sweetness to remain and kind words to heed.

Growing old, grace when applied lavishly is more
Brilliant and beautiful than all the ages precede.

The Sea

The vast and majestic sea,
It stirs something in the depth of me.
It calls out to my spirit deep within,
The crashing waves and the salty wind.
The soft, warm sand beneath my feet,
The call of the seagull sounds so sweet.
I stand amazed looking at the beautiful blue hues,
Endless and magnificent as my love for you.

My Heart Cries

My heart is crying for my lack;
Was our love ever on track?

Will Your love ever be mine,
Dazzling, sparkling like new wine?

Please don't hide Your love from me;
I'm hopeless, helpless, can't you see?

Thirsty is my love for You;
Quench it, pour it out, sweet and true.

Let Your love take this ache away;
Sweetly, kindly, bring it to stay.

Can't you see I'm slowly dying inside;
Without Your love, my heart cries.

I feel like I'm about to take flight
Away, away into the night.

When my heart is ravaged by sin, don't walk away;
Hold me help me, please stay.

Is there no love like this to be found?
Yes, at Calvary, His love flowed down.

Connection

Who do you connect with when it's a dark and dreary land?
Is it your faith or your feelings that take a stand?
Doubt and despair will drag you down into a hole;
Faith and hope will keep you standing solid and whole.
Feelings are deceptive, they change with the wind;
One moment you're happy, the next you're guilty of sin.
Faith is the key that ushers in God's grace;
Hope keeps your focus and gives you strength to run the race.
Let your connection be faith in God's word and love;
He will shower down blessings on the wings of a dove.

Tim

In the darkness of the night, when sleep will not come,
The demons torment and accuse until the morning sun.
The pain and suffering does not pass;
Am I to live in this misery? Will it always last?
I pray and believe, but the answer does not come;
I'm crying out and hoping for a touch from God's Son.
Sift me like Job and purify my heart;
I need a new life, and I long for a new start,
Patience and endurance are what I've acquired;
I long in Your Spirit to go deeper and higher.
When will my healing come? In hope, I do ask;
The loving touch of Your hand is Your willing task.
Father, please, keep Your eyes on me
and keep me in your sight;
I long to be free of pain and soar to new heights.
I'm hanging on to faith and hope, and I will not let go
Until Your healing love on me comes with evidence to show.
In this refiner's fire, God surely worked His will;
Purification and sanctification makes for others I deeply feel.
A testing of great magnitude
will bring mighty glory to God's Son;
He's trustworthy, faithful, and lovely—the Three in One.

The Vastness of the Sea

The vastness of the sea,
Oh how it thrills me.
To see the seagulls fly,
to hear their shrill cries.
To feel the wind on my face,
My lips do love that salty taste.
To hear the crashing of the waves,
To see the rising, misty haze.
The vastness of the sea,
Oh how it thrills me.
To dig my feet into the sand,
How the waves rise to kiss the land.
The beauty of the ocean,
and the setting sun.
Thanking God for this pleasure,
My heart He has won.

Arms of Grace

I fell into His arms of grace;
Oh, what comfort and care.
He held me close to His heart of love;
His healing mercies were there.

His arms of grace, so pure and sweet;
His love washed through my soul.
My grateful heart, so humble and clean;
His cleansing blood made me whole.

I fell into His arms of grace;
My wretched heart made new.
By His tender love and truth,
My life in Jesus grew.

Now I have arms of grace;
For All who have pain come near.
I'll love, comfort, and care for you
And pray away your fears
And wipe away your tears.

God's Love

You're every love I've ever known;
My strongest love clearly shown.
You're a father's love that's strong and sure;
A mother's love that's tender and pure.
You're a brother's love that's protective and strong,
A sister's love that sees no wrong,
A friend's love that's there at all times,
And a husband's love that faithfully shines.
You're every love I've ever known,
And so much more than any shown.

Home

I'm so happy that I'm home in heaven;
My tears and pain are gone.
The light and beauty of his presence
Fills my heart with a song.
I'll always love and miss you,
But I know it won't be long
Before we meet together again
With all fear and sadness gone.
Please continue to fight the battles
And run the race to win;
Jesus has given you the strength
And conquered death and sin.
Remember, I am with you;
In your heart, I'll always be.
For love in Christ is forever;
In Him we are happy and free.

The Gentleman

He strolled into my life with that shy, flirty grin;
It didn't take long before he was my best friend.

We played and talked like the day had no end;
It didn't take long before he was more than a friend.

Our love grew, and its tender shoots we did tend.
It didn't take long before he was my dear love,
more than a friend.

Dance With Me, Jesus

Dance with me, Jesus, as the morning light appears;
Through the day I need you close to wipe away the tears.
Hold me tight in laughter, in sorrow, and in pain;
In Your strong embrace, I will always remain.
Let me hear Your heartbeat as I press against Your breast;
Let my heart beat in tune as in Your arms I rest.
Dance with me, Jesus, as the evening stars shine bright;
Being in Your arms is my perfect delight.

His Love

His love, nothing can be compared;
It consumes me like a fire.
The depth of that love constantly
Takes me so much higher.
It's sweeter than the finest wine;
No matter where you search, you cannot find.
It's a gift of love that comes rushing in
When you open your heart to this Savior and friend.
It's a love that calms the raging in me;
It provides peace deep within me.
His love will never end;
It will be poured out, watered, and tend.
His love was found at Calvary's tree
Poured out for you and me.

Give it Away

The world pulls our hearts in so many different ways;
The treasure of this earth will rob all our days.
Don't you know your money has little value until given away?
We cannot serve both God and money; only one can stay.
When we empty ourselves of all these temporal things,
A happiness and joy will fill us
that only the Holy Spirit can bring.
Kindly bless those around you
that are struggling in their needs;
Jesus will richly bless you for His word you did heed.
So turn your whole heart to Jesus and let him have control;
Wisdom will find you and your light will be bold.

Goodbye for Now

For you, my love,
I fought with all my heart and soul;
But now it won't be long before
the Savior's face I will behold.
The battle was long and hard,
and the tears I could not hide;
Stealing extra moments was worth it all with you by my side.
I loved you complete, I loved you thorough,
I loved you with all I had,
So when I leave, please be happy remembering,
please don't be sad.
It won't be long till we're together again,
for now the children and grandchildren please care;
Goodbye my dear, I'll be waiting for you—
a wonderful reunion we will share.

Daddy's Hands

I hold tight my daddy's hand all along the way;
I hold tight my daddy's hand when I sing and dance and play.
I hold tight my daddy's hand when the clouds roll into my day;
My daddy holds tight my hand
when my little feet want to stray.
My daddy holds tight my hand until I yield and want to stay;
We hold each other's hand as we fellowship, love, and pray.

Holiness

Holiness is what I want, Lord
Walking upright with Thee;
Without spot or wrinkle
Holy in You, walking free.
When others walk in the gray
And compromise is all around,
Pull me up and away.
In You my life is found;
Holiness is my hearts deepest desire,
To be hide in You and go deeper and higher.

Passion Found

My mom and dad were humble and poor;
We loved Jesus with an open door.
Family alters and prayer was a part of what we did;
Church and bible study, there was no goodness that we hid.
Like the Pharisees, the mezuzah was in place;
To the synagogue we did make haste.
Whitewashed, all the rules we did keep;
A good reputation we did seek.
Kathryn Kuhlman, Oral, Billy Graham, we all took in;
We were Christian of Christians with just as much sin.
Yes Christian of Christians and one of the best;
Studied with Copeland, Haggard, and all of the rest.
ORU was the school Christians all went;
Even to the Hebrew University a group of us was sent.
I'll go into every man's world you'll see,
Preaching, prophesying—grand miracles there'll be.
Camp counselor, mission trips,
Bunch Indian outreach was grand.
But was I personal with Jesus? Where did He stand?
I married the best and noblest of all,
An ORU athlete—handsome, kind, and tall.
We were leaders and elders everywhere we went;
A sweet family who touched many wherever we were sent.
The enemy did trip us up a few times or two,
But we triumphed over him like good Christians do.
The children are all raised—we're proud of all of them;
In my crown, they are my gems.
Nurses, doctors, author and more,
Professor, security guard—these I adore.
A Pharisee of Pharisees, no that's not what I've been;
A Christian of Christians with just as much sin.
My road to Damascus in the blinding light.
I saw the truth, and it was an awful sight.

Although the performance had been grand,
Jesus wants intimacy, not clapping hands.
Jesus wants our hearts and all of it,
Not Pharisee deeds and little tidbits.
Don't let religion use you up with its business and good deeds;
Jesus wants time with you, His word to heed.
A life of love and sharing Jesus is what we need,
Not competing to see who the next elder will be.
Now loving Jesus is what I'm all about;
Loving the least of the least and giving it all,
Makes my heart happy and makes it shout.
Prayer is the key I've been looking for;
Intimacy with Jesus is what I adore.
Agape love now fills my soul;
For intimacy with Jesus, I am made whole.

Granny Annie

Granny puts the teddy bear right next to my chest
So I can cuddle and hug it while I get my rest.

Granny always likes to do fun things with me;
She likes to watch me play and climb the big birch tree.

Granny takes me for long walks
so the beautiful sunset I can see;
Walking and singing with granny makes me happy as can be.

Granny likes to talk about all the things Mommy did;
It's fun to learn about Mommy when she was just a kid.

Granny's house is so much fun;
I can play with the doggies and swim in the sun.

I love to go to Granny's—
it makes my little heart soar
Because I know Granny loves me so much and even more.

Granny teaches me all about art and poetry,
Then she lets me sneak some candy and drink sweet tea.

Granny likes to pray for me; her faith is very strong.
She says Jesus loves me so much; He forgives all my wrong.

Granny is my best friend;
I'll miss her when she's gone,
But in my heart she'll always be with a special song.

You Saw My Heart

I was the one that didn't stand
When the preacher said, "Raise your hand."

I didn't move, I didn't dare;
My heart was pounding, and I felt sort of scared.

He asked if we wanted Jesus and all to respond;
You saw my heart—
I wanted that bond.

You reached down and touched me
even though I couldn't move;
You said that didn't matter—
I had nothing to prove.

A peace settled on me and my fears all melted away;
You said You'd never leave me,
and in my heart You'd always stay.

Prayers for my Children

Lord, I don't understand why my prayers
were answered in such ways;
Regardless of the outcome,
my trust in You will stay.
Pain and trauma I prayed against
did come into my children's life;
Perhaps they need to see Your grace and mercy
covers any failure, sin, or strife.
I always want the very best for my children
without pain or sorrow;
Tribulation produces character in our life for today
and will benefit tomorrow.
You promised to complete the good work in them,
and they would be mighty in the Land,
Pain and brokenness softens our hearts
and then we're shaped by your hand.
To bring hope and healing to all we meet,
Then Your plans for us will be complete.

My Prayer to Thee

Oh Lord, reveal Yourself to me in the abundance
of Your grace and glory;
Let Your hidden life in me be my blessed story.
Come to me, Lord, in my humble, broken state.
By the Holy Spirit work; use me now, not late.
Teach me always, Oh Lord, to know Your will;
To hear Your sweet voice, and my heart be stilled.
Oh Lord, my heart is broken and contrite
for all the failure and sin of my life;
I lay it down at Your feet as my best sacrifice.
By night or day, in life or death, may I always be true to Thee;
Oh Lord of my heart, my faithful friend,
my risen Savior in Your hands I will always be.
Oh Lord, open my eyes to see
the treasure and the riches of Your Holy Word;
In Your secret place of love my life is safely gird.

Used by God

God is an awesome creator,
perfect in His giving of gifts;
We should expect them and use them
for others to bless and lift.
Don't judge or cast away the perfect gifts that He gives;
Take off the cover of selfishness
and beneath we are splendor to live.
Hiding your light under a bushel is weak and wrong;
Let the Holy Spirit build you up and in Him be strong.
There is no greater joy then to be used by God's hand
Serving and giving and helping others to stand.

In My Heart

I hold you in my heart always,
And my prayers are always near
To comfort you in your sorrows
And wipe away the tears.
I'll be here for you in the morning
And in the noonday sun;
Here for you as the evening sets
And night has just begun.
I hold you in my heart always,
And my prayers will always be near
To keep away the troubles and hold back the fears.
I'll be happy when you're happy,
And I'll weep when you cry;
I'll be here from beginning to end,
And I'll hold you when you die.
I'll hold you in my heart always,
Death can't separate our love;
For it has been a rare treasure
Showered down from heaven above.

Tapestry

Our life is like a tapestry God's hand has woven in place;
Each thread is woven in by His mercy and His grace,
The colors are so beautiful, the pattern is just right.
It all seems to shimmer and shine when it's in the light.
There is a thread of crimson red that was woven
through and through;
It was woven between all the colors,
the greens, yellows, and blues.
The colors of the green represent
the fullness of His life in me;
His sacrifice and mercy have set my soul free.
The yellow is His fullness of joy of a life lived in Him;
Full happiness and peace and His covering of sin.
Blue steadfastness He gives through the trials of life;
Holy Spirit always present to cleanse and rid strife.
The pain and suffering of my life made a unique design;
It captures your focus for the thread is delicate and fine.
The one thread that holds it all in place is the crimson red;
It represents the cross of Christ on which He died and bled.
Now the tapestry is beautiful and the pattern complete;
Because of that one crimson red, I'll lay it at his feet.

Happiness

Happiness in its truest form
Is a budding rose and a baby born;
It's watching the bluebird on the windowsill rest,
And it's angels carrying you home soon after death.
Happiness is anticipation of the good things to come,
Like kissing the face of your new grandson.
Happiness is sitting with a sweet old man,
and hearing of times past,
Pure, simple, and true where a handshake of integrity did last.
Happiness is sweet memories of times past,
For the moment is fleeting; it does not last.
Happiness is a friend's smiling hello
And watching the beauty of winter's first snow.
Happiness is knowing your well-loved,
And when you close your eyes, there is a home above.
Happiness is knowing the Savior
And knowing you're in His favor.

Full

When you're full of Jesus,
Your trials fade into His light.
It does not matter the challenges,
His presence covers the night.
So I press into His life,
Where sweet intimacy will be.
You'll be so spiritually full
That a multitude you'll feed.

Knight in Shining Armor

You are my knight in shining armor;
You came for me just in time.
You defeated all my enemies and You became mine.
It's not just a fairy tale;
My knight in shining armor caught me as I fell.
This true story I do tell;
Your strong arm of deliverance swept me off my feet.
The enemy's pursuing me, but Your love did defeat.
Now You're carrying me on this journey towards home;
Forever in Your arms of love never more to roam.
Fighting every battle, I'm safe in Your strong arms,
Sheltered from the enemy's deceit, lies, and harm.
My knight in shining armor
will carry me into our castle in the sky;
Forever to be loved by Him, no more tears to cry.

Boundaries

The depth of a person you do not know;
Only Holy Spirit looks deep into the soul.
He's the only one who can truly see;
He's the only one who fashioned you and me.
So trust the Lord in others' lives;
Crossing the boundaries only brings strife.
Holy Spirit is gentle and kind;
He will do His work at just the right time.

Quiet

Sitting quiet in Your presence;
Your peace fills my soul.
The cares of the world fade,
And I am made whole.
Sitting in Your presence,
Your face in my sight;
My spirit is filled with Your Holy light.
Sitting quiet in Your presence
Gives a soft and tender heart.
Receiving all Your love for me
That You gently impart.
Sitting quiet in Your presence,
I'm focused and clearly see.
It's intimacy with You,
And building the kingdom for eternity.

Only God

Only God can change a heart and look deep into the soul;
You can only see the outward, you cannot make one whole.
We think we have all this knowledge and wisdom to share,
But take a look at Yourself in the mirror, there's a lot to care.
The secret judgments that you have will only do you harm;
Your attitude can't hide it or cover it with charm.
So humble yourselves and bow to the cross,
the Lord will meet you there;
Then with love and grace You'll have sweetness to share.

Deep Desire

Knowing Christ is my deepest heart's desire;
I want to be in that abiding place
where His love takes me higher.
I long for total intimacy, His life in mine;
I know in that place of love, His light will fully shine.
I want to walk as He walks, obedient in trust and faith,
And talk as He talks, always full of grace.

Teach Me

Father, teach me to stop for the one,
To look into their face,
To have compassion on their needs,
And run with them this race.
Father, teach me to live in the moment,
To forget about the past,
And to trust You for the future;
For the time is passing too fast.
Father, teach me to love deeply,
And Holy Spirit fill my soul,
To walk in Your footsteps always
Where Your blood has made us whole

Your Face

When I look into Your lovely face,
Songs of deliverance fill my soul;
Your blood washes over me,
Cleansing and making me whole.
When I look into Your face of love,
Your peace and grace enter in
Bringing calm, trust, and faith
And cleansing every sin.
When I look into Your sweet, sweet face,
Your love melts my heart;
Your joy and refreshment invades me,
Entering every part.
When I look into Your lovely face,
I see eyes of the purest love,
Affirming me, accepting me,
And holding me as a gentle dove.

A Healing God

He healed my heart,
He healed my soul,
He healed my body,
And He made me whole.
Cast your cares,
He'll gladly bear;
In pain and suffering,
He'll see you through.
He's always watching out for you.
It may seem impossible,
For the valley is so deep.
Your eyes have gone dry
For all the tears that you weep.
He bottles them all up
And holds them close to His heart.
He knows when the answer will come
And gives a fresh start.
Wait patiently and trust
His hand of mercy and grace;
For the day will soon come
(and be worth it all)
As we see Him face to face.

El Morro Bay

Thank You, Lord, for this beautiful day
that You show in every way;
Thank You for the beauty in the sky
and all the colors that shine so high.
Thank You for the diverse foliage and trees so green;
Everywhere you look, beauty is to be seen.
Thank You for the mighty ocean
that highlights all the colors of blue;
The mighty waves that crash in sparkling hues.
Thank You for the warm sand beneath my toes,
And all the sand dollars that it shows.
Thank You for the seagulls that caw praises to You
With majestic flight through morning fog and dew.
Thank You for El Morro Rock, towering above the sea
And reminding me of Your great love and mercy for me.
Thank You for Morro Bay and the beauty that is told;
The wildlife sanctuary and all creatures that it holds.
Thank You for the otters and seals playing
 so gracefully in the waves,
But more than anything,
Thank You for Jesus dying on the cross for me to save!

A Mother's Prayer

My heart is weeping, though no tears flow;
The bonds of his love, his life does not show.
Sorrow and pleading, my soul does cry;
Please God, my son, my son, I don't want to die.
Bruised, broken, and wounded, he does go;
Save him, heal him, Your love please show.
Tormented and lonely, looking for a light;
In Your mercy and grace, You showed up in the night.
His dream was sweet and gentle,
inviting him, please don't run.
I have a good plan for you in the love of my Son.
He died to set you free and fill your lonely soul;
Just follow me and I'll lead you
to God's goal and make you whole.
Holy Spirit please help him to respond to that gentle plea;
For Your love and grace will set him free.

Daddy's Lap

Crawling up in Daddy's lap,
His peace does flood my soul;
He holds me with His tender arms,
His touch does make me whole.
Crawling up in Daddy's lap,
He sings softly of His love
With His voice so sweet and descending
Like a snow-white dove.
Crawling up in Daddy's lap
I'm safe from raging storms;
Hearing His heartbeat,
I'm safe and warm.
He hides me in His strong embrace,
His goodness and mercy
I do taste.
Crawling up in Daddy's lap,
My soul finds perfect rest;
Loving Daddy
And lying on His breast.

Did You Know?

Did you know the tests you go through
Become sweet testimonies to the keeping grace of God?
They're not forgotten, hidden, or lost in a fog.
Did you know the trials you go through
Become mighty triumphs of God's mercy and love?
Through them we are showered with perseverance from above.
Did you know the messes you go through
Become powerful messages of God's tender care?
In them, you learn to wait, to trust, and to others share.
You see, your test becomes a testimony;
Your trial becomes a triumph.
Your mess becomes a message
When you put your faith and hope in God's love.
You're not a victim but a victor
With the Holy Spirit coming upon you from above.

I Learned

I learned the light was to see
Others needs and lives, not just about me.
I learned in the dark not to grope,
But to trust, laced with hope.
I learned in the sunshine to sing;
Much joy to others it does bring.
I learned the rain was to dance
Like children who splash and prance;
I learned when it's noisy to disappear
Into our hiding place
Where there is no fear
I learned in the quiet to listen
With heart and ears;
It's there I feel God's presence
And His voice so clear.

Balm in Gilead

There is a balm in Gilead
Running from Emanuel's veins;
The precious blood of Jesus
Covering my grief and pain.
There is a balm in Gilead
That soothes the hurting soul;
His comforting arms round me
Heals my wounded soul.
There is a balm in Gilead
For all to partake;
Just turn your eyes to Jesus
And all else forsake.
There is a balm in Gilead
Where hope has its gain,
And all our loved ones sing and dance,
Where Jesus rules and reigns.

Thank You, Lord

Thank You for the beautiful sunrise and the soft morning dew;
The colors of the sky, such radiant hues.
Thank You for the winter snow
that reminds us of your cleansing blood
Washing over us as a raging flood.
Thank You for the budding trees
and the business of the bees,
Celebrating spring and all the joy it brings.
Thank You for the freshness of the gentle rain
Watering all the flowers for the beauty that is gained.
Thank You for the rays of the warm summer sun
and the growth it brings,
Causing celebrations and our hearts to sing.
Thank You for the magic of trees turning gold,
All the oranges, yellows, reds come on so bold.
Thank You for it all, Lord,
the vast beauty not all told,
The mountain peaks, the oceans deep, the valleys so low.
The love You show in all creation brings such delight;
It touches deep inside;
Your beauty shines so bright.

The Cross

Lay me at The Cross,
I don't care the cost.
I need to behold Your face
Wrapped by Your arms of grace.
Lay me at The Cross
All the worldliness I toss;
Your life in me, my desire.
Take me deeper, take me higher.
Lay me at The Cross
Here I will bow low
For Your love to show.

All of Heaven Weeps

All of Heaven weeps looking down upon our broken Earth;
God's dear sacrifice was given for a new birth.
Weeping for the old man lying in the slum;
And weeping for the teen running with a gun.
Weeping for the babies dying in their mothers' wombs;
They thought it was safe, but it became a tomb.
Weeping for the widow forgotten and placed away;
She thought with her children, she would always stay.
Weeping for the black person, Jew,
and Native American treated so unfair;
They just wanted to live in peace
and for their families care.
Weeping for the families broken and in pain;
Jesus brings peace and in Him much gain.
Weeping for all the pain and suffering His children do bear;
His hands of grace and mercy extending with love and care.
All of Heaven weeps for the sin upon the Earth;
Heaven sent the very best, God's Son,
to die for sin and give new birth.
Heaven weeps for those who turn away
this precious gift and reject;
Weeping for those in eternity holding such regret.
Heaven weeps.

You are Good, Lord!

I will praise You in my suffering;
I will praise You in my pain
Because You are good, Lord,
You are good!
I will praise You in the sunshine,
I will praise You in the rain
Because you are good, Lord,
You are good!
I will praise You as my heart weeps,
I will praise You when I can't sleep
Because You are good, Lord,
You are good!
I will praise You in my victories,
I will praise You in defeat
Because You are good, Lord,
You are good!
I will praise You if healing does not come,
I will praise you when my days are done
Because You are good Lord
You are good!

Those I Love

See the tears for those I love Lord,
Those I cherish and adore.
Hear the prayers I pray for them;
Convict, cleanse, and enter in.
They are hurting, lost, and in pain;
Abba, cover and heal them, their need so plain.
Turn their hearts complete to You;
Heal body, soul, and mind renew.
Complete Your good work in them,
They are my gifts, my friends.
Polish them so they will shine
In Your love a new life to find.

Goodbye

Saying goodbye is never easy,
So I'll say so long for now.
In God's grace and mercy,
He will show me how.
Our days together have been many,
And all the love, we've shared
Will always be in my heart, for you I deeply cared.
For me you were always there.
You were the wind beneath my sails,
The one with whom I could share.
I won't say goodbye because
In my heart you'll always be
So long for now, but together
Again throughout eternity.

He's Everywhere

He's in the clouds drifting by,
He's in the blue hues of the sky.
He's in the softness of the breeze,
He's in the swaying of the leaves.
He's in the songs of the locust in the trees.
He's in everything and everywhere,
In you and me.
He's in the stars, sun, and moon.
He's in every song and every tune.
He's in the crashing of the waves.
He's in the softness of the sand.
Yet, He's so intimate, He'll hold you in His hand.

Silent Tears

My hear tis crying silent tears
For all the pain, suffering and fears,
For those babies who will not live,
Their mothers would not give,
The homeless man in despair,
People who do not care,
For the suffering with disease and pain.
In Your grace, let them find gain.
Oh God, Oh God, my heart breaks in two
For this hurting world if only they could see You.
Our children who have lost their way,
The husbands who would not stay,
Silent tears day and night,
Intercession is my fight.
May all I do share your love and light,
Silent tears day and night,
Intercession is this fight.

The Line

There is a line being drawn in the sand,
You are going to have to take a stand.
There is so much injustice in the land,
Babies being murdered in their mother's womb,
Black people trampled on and put in a tomb.
We must take a stand and hold justice and
Righteousness in our hand.
Don't listen to enticements with corruption and lies,
Seek truth in God's word and righteousness
With nothing to hide.
There is a line being drawn in the sand,
For truth and righteousness you must take a stand.
Jesus is the way, the truth and the life,
For these values you must fight.
You must choose to support,
If not, you'll see integrity along with babies continue to abort.

Fall

The beauty of Fall surrounds me,
The colors brilliantly shine.
The leaves are dancing praises
To Thee as the light touches the dying vine.
Looking up into the heavens,
A grateful heart sips new wine.
The trees wave their goodbyes,
As the leaves take their flight.
Dancing praises to Thee with harmony and delight.

Extended Mercy

Extended mercy is here today,
Fear and doubt is melting away.
Goodness and mercy is here to stay.
Extended mercy keeps me going strong.
Stepping over all the wrong.
His grace has kept me all along.
Extended mercy keeps me giving to all,
Holding them up so they won't fall,
Encouraging to hear the Lord's call.
Extended mercy is God's goodness to me.
His love I so plainly see.
In His sweet presence I'll always be,
In His extended mercy.

Surrendered

There is a call so deep where my heart is totally given,
All my life and desire is Holy Spirit driven.
The word becomes my food,
Holy Spirit, my teacher, and guide.
In His sweet presence I live, move, and abide.
The overflow has power, the miracles do show,
Many are delivered, their lives made whole.
The price is total surrender, in Holy Spirit, I hide.
All power and authority is given walking by His side.

Like the Waves

Like the waves of the ocean,
Sparkling beauty in the sunlight,
More radiant and pure in the misty moonlight.
The waves roll in and kiss the shore,
Sharing their treasures from the ocean floor.
Here with your kindness and then no more,
Waves with sorrow roll back to sea
Into the depths with a silent plea.
Gone with no voice, your burdens you bear,
I want to encourage you, your troubles to share.
You're like the waves of the ocean,
Sparkling beauty in sunlight;
When you leave, it's the dark of night.

Breath of Heaven

The enemy is snuffing out God's breath upon the Earth,
All of nature groans for new birth.
Heaven and Earth is passing away,
Makes my heart mourn,
The breath of heaven will be restored to its perfect form.
God's beautiful creation was for us to care,
Our sin and selfishness stripped it bare.
Our hope is in heaven and God alone,
He restores all things to his perfect form.
Breathe in the breath of Heaven,
And let joy fill your soul.
Holy Spirit energizes, making all whole.

Thin Places

Thin places is where I always want to be;
Wrapped in Your arms of grace,
Leaning on thee.
The thin places I commune and walk
With my Father God.
Stepping out of all the worldly fog,
He fills me up with His love and life
To pour out to others healing sin and strife.
Thin places are all around,
Be quiet and listen, you can hear their sound.
Connecting us to that heavenly place,
Touching Him, receiving pure grace.
I cultivate my life around the thin place of prayer.
Then I'm always ready, the gospel to share.

Smile at Me

Smile at me when I am gone,
As you gaze at the beauty of the rising sun.
Smile at me in the noonday light
When victories heart has won.
Smile at me when sunset hues streak across the sky,
Sharing its love and beauty in us does abide.
Smile at me when the midnight moon is
Shining bright and high.
Breathing in its deep peace with a hopeful sigh.
Smile at me when thinking of us walking
Barefoot on the sand.
Close we walked hand in hand.
Smile while looking up at me knowing my
Heart will always be yours eternally.

I Love

I love to watch the birthing of spring,
To my soul such joy it brings.
One day it's bare, the next it's green.
I love to watch the birds singing as building their nest;
All nature is awake from the long winter's rest.
I love to watch the clouds floating by
As the budding leaves wave hello,
And watching the beautiful sunset with its magical glow.
I love to watch the awakening of spring
With all the magic and beauty it brings.

66995029R00065